Come Meet

A How-To Biblical Retreat/Study Guide for Women

Bette Decoteau

WestBow
PRESS
A DIVISION OF THOMAS NELSON
& ZONDERVAN

WestBow Press books may be ordered through booksellers or by contacting:

WestBow Press
A Division of Thomas Nelson & Zondervan
1663 Liberty Drive
Bloomington, IN 47403
www.westbowpress.com
1 (866) 928-1240

ISBN: 978-1-4908-8552-0 (sc)
ISBN: 978-1-4908-8551-3 (e)

Library of Congress Control Number: 2015910085

Print information available on the last page.

WestBow Press rev. date: 7/2/2015

Contents

Brief Description of Proposed Book, Unique Contribution, and Why It Should Be Published

This book will help women study groups or retreat leaders with subjects and a course of action. The goal is to keep it concise, uncomplicated, and inexpensive so even small groups can participate. These studies can be used individually or as part of a series. There are specific guidelines as to minute-by-minute schedules, songs and/or videos, worship subjects, and conclusions that can be followed exactly or adapted by a particular group. It can be used by large or small churches and provides the right blend of teaching and creativity. The suggested retreat or study includes a perfect combination of reverence, levity, and learning for a women's program.

Intended Reader

The intended reader is a pastor or women's group leaders who desire to create an interesting, inspirational study with a few hours of fun and sharing among the women of their community. It can be accomplished on a shoestring budget or as part of an elaborate women's luncheon.

About the Author

My personal bio sketch is as follows: Bette A. Decoteau, Wales, Massachusetts, and Naples, Florida. I graduated magna cum with a bachelor's in religion from Liberty University in Lynchburg, Virginia, in 2012. I was baptized and accepted Christ as my Savior at the age of twelve in my hometown. At the age of nineteen, I married my husband Hank, a military man, and we spent the next ten years traveling around the world. After he had served twenty years in the military, we retired to Martha's Vineyard and hoped to live there for what we thought would be forever. It turned out to be only twenty years because God had other plans for us. We have taken care of children, aging parents, and now ourselves, sharing time between Massachusetts and Florida. I am currently serving as Associate Lay Pastor at Mayflower UCC in Naples, Florida. I wrote the verbiage for these retreats. However, it takes several women to accomplish the event, so I'd like to thank the women of Mayflower UCC for making these retreats possible and successful. I'd like to dedicate this book to Pastor Judy Montgomery, who went home to glory about a month after meeting Mary and Martha.

Introduction

Welcome, church and lay leaders. This book is intended to provide a step-by-step, comprehensive how-to guide for Christian women's group leaders and retreat organizers. It can be used by any size group of women seeking to learn more about some women of the Bible.

Thinking about a retreat or a study of women in the Bible? You can do it with any group, and budgets can vary from shoestring to carte blanche. This book will outline the needs of the study, from personnel to supplies, and contains program scripts, which of course you are free to modify depending on your size. There is a basic agenda set where there is a group worship, prayer, and introduction time. Then part of the day will be broken up into individual discussion groups. A good group size comes in multiples of six or seven. If that doesn't work, try to keep individual table groups over four to allow for active participation. After the discussion time, there will be interaction within the entire group and final devotion.

You will need to schedule a training session for your table leaders a couple of days to a week before the event. This will be a time to go over the questions and helpful hints. Get them the material ahead of time so they can prepare their questions. There should be enough helps so leading isn't a great burden on the table leaders as most of their work is done for them.

This book will outline the program study with word-by-word directions. However, you will need to review and select songs or videos that your organization team thinks are important or familiar to your particular group. I have made suggestions, but you may want to tailor them.

Set-Up, Logistics, and Fees

The first order of business is always to pray. Pray that this is something that God is leading you to do in your church or community of women.

A team of five or six is about right for the organization team of the retreat. Keep in mind that you will need table leaders and that number will be determined by a preregistration or guesstimate. Table leaders don't necessarily have to be part of the organization team, but if you have a small group, they can be both. It would be helpful to have someone who is knowledgeable in technology. If your church has audio/visual equipment with Internet access, wonderful, but if not a laptop or desktop computer will work. If you have no access to any of this equipment then someone with music ability is essential.

Call an organizational meeting and hand out this workbook to each team member. Decide which of the three women groups you want to study, set a date for your retreat, and give yourselves a minimum of one month to plan.

You will need to decide if you want to include lunch or not. This will of course affect the cost of the retreat.

Using clip art, pictures, or some other likeness, find a logo and write up and print invitations using a home or church printer. From the church or ladies group membership list, make labels for the women only, and prepare them so they can be sent out about three weeks ahead. The invitation should be fairly plain, with the logo on the outside and the date, times, and location on the inside with an invitational statement like, "Come meet Mary and Martha." Use part of the selected Scripture (i.e., for Martha & Mary use Luke 10:41: "'Martha, Martha,' the Lord answered, 'You are worried and upset about many things, but only one thing is needed. Mary has chosen what is better, and it will not be taken away from her.'"). Divide the completed invitations up, and give each member of the team several to sign so they all have a salutation and signature from someone on the committee. This gives it a personal touch and encourages the women to think that someone really wants them to come.

It is beneficial to have a place to hold the retreat where there are two different areas, such as a meeting hall and a sanctuary. It gives people a chance to move around and food can be served or cleared away without interrupting the worship parts of the retreat.

The meeting/greeting room should be set up with a sign-in table, comfortable tables and chairs to share coffee, and a breakfast table for muffins, breads, or doughnuts. Plan for the team to be there about 8:00 a.m. to get the room set up. Begin registration about nine, with an informal get-together. Each registrant will be given a packet with the itinerary and event booklet and a name tag with the table assignment. Randomly separate people who come together so the women will have to mingle with people they don't know. Fees can be collected at this time. A little before nine thirty, ask everyone to proceed into the sanctuary. Make sure someone from your team stays behind to cover the food, clear the debris, and make sure the tables are ready for discussion time.

A good sound system and microphone are imperative. A portable mic is great so all the women can participate without having to get up from their seats. If you have a small group, make sure you sit close so everyone can hear and respond.

Fees should be charged to cover the costs of the packets, printing, refreshments, etc. Later in the book there will be a list and some rough estimates about items to be secured or purchased. A good, economical number to charge is about ten dollars per person. That should cover expenses.

Packet folders can be purchased at any office supply or big bulk store. They can be just cardboard with side pouches and run about fifty cents each. Watch sales because sometimes you can get them cheaper or can be bulk purchased through the church.

Even *event booklets* can be printed just about anywhere. It is most efficient to use something like 10" x 17" to get four pages in one printing and they can be folded in the center. These booklets should contain an agenda, pertinent Scriptures, songs (if hymnals aren't available), group discussion questions, and if space allows, a few blank sheet for notes.

Blank paper and envelopes can go in one of the pockets for the "self letter time" if your group decides to do something like that. *Name tags and labels for the packet cover* can be printed from any printer on label stock, and 2" x 3" work best

Make a *questionnaire* with a *few* basic questions to help your group evaluate the things you did well and the things that could be done better (sample on the next page).

Food

These numbers are based on a sample group of fifty people and estimated costs are as follows:

- Sending about one hundred invitations with envelopes: $150
- Packet and event booklets: $100
- Name tags and folder labels: $25
- Food for morning and simple lunch: $225
- Total: $500

If you charge ten dollars each, you have broken even, and if you watch your sales and put a donation jar around the food table, you may even have a little left over for some specialties, such as laminated bookmarkers with the logo picture and Scripture. This makes a nice gift, and to print fifty it costs approximately thirty dollars.

Questionnaire

1. What did you like best about this morning's activities?

   _____

2. What did you like least about this morning's activities?

   _____

3. What would you like to do differently?

   _____

4. What other women would you like to study?

   _____

Come Meet
Mary and Martha

Welcome to the study of Martha and Mary. This is intended to inspire women to understand themselves and how they relate to these biblical sisters. We use several reference guides, such as: *NIV Study Bible*[1] and *Women of the Bible*.[2]

This study can be used by groups of any size. It is designed for women to learn and share in a limited amount of time (three to four hours) but can be adapted to stretch into a full day by adding a lunch and lengthening discussion times. It allows for creativity, sharing, reflection, and spiritual education.

Organizers are encouraged to get guest speakers or singers, use electronics, and/or stick to basics and sing the old familiar hymns. Leaders have the freedom to tailor the study to their own groups and yet share the blessings of the biblical message of Martha and Mary.

---

[1] Copyright 1973, 1978, 1984 by International Bible Society. Zondervan Publishing, Grand Rapids, Michigan.
[2] Ann Spangler and Jean E. Syswerda, *Women of the Bible.* (Grand Rapids, MI: Zondervan Publishing, 1999).

Agenda

To dress it up, use whatever you pick for a logo and
Luke 10:41: "'Martha, Martha,' the Lord answered, 'You are worried
and upset about many things, but only one thing is needed. Mary has
chosen what is better, and it will not be taken away from her.'"

9:00–9:30: Welcome, coffee, registration—relax and enjoy greeting everyone

9:30–9:45: Opening, introduction, and praise in the sanctuary (if possible)

9:45–10:15: Scriptures and reflection

10:15–11:00: Small work groups

11:00–11:30: Group presentations, sharing, and summation

11:40–11:50: Short motivational woman speaker (or two)

12:00–12:15: Letter-writing time and/or private devotional time

12:15–12:30: Conclusion, praise songs, and prayer

Martha and Mary

9:30–9:45: Opening, introduction, and praise in the sanctuary (if possible). *You need a leader for this.*

Welcome, ladies, to the first of what we hope will be many women's retreats at our church. To get us off on the right foot, let us pray. "Father God, we gather here as women seeking to learn more about You and Your servants, Mary and Martha. We ask You to bless us, help us to leave the world outside, and let us feel Your presence this morning in this place. In Jesus' name, amen."

Now let's open with a song. If you know it, help us sing! Remember these are praise songs, so don't be afraid to get loud, clap, or raise your hands. Be happy this is our time to put everything aside except the Spirit. Let Him come and give us what we need.

Everyone on the team should go up front to sing "Here I Am to Worship."

Housekeeping Announcements, Folder Instruction, and Scheduling

This morning we pray that we will gain a better understanding of the lessons God wants us to learn from Martha and Mary. Before we get started, we have a few housekeeping and scheduling items to deal with. When you registered, you were given a packet. Inside you should have a schedule for this morning and the Scripture we are basing our study on. A questionnaire is also included for you to fill out at the end of the day to help us plan for the next retreat. Let us know what you liked and what you didn't like. We want you to tell all. How can we do this better?

On the other side of the folder is a piece of paper and an envelope. If you look at the schedule, you can see this will be used to write yourself a letter, which the committee will mail back to you in a few months. It will be whatever you want to remember about this day or say to yourself about the experience you've had this morning. Put that in the back of your mind for later.

Bathrooms are located _____.

The committee has worked very hard on this agenda, and we hope to keep to the times as much as possible. We invite you to stay for a short lunch after the retreat. Without further ado, let's get this amazing day started.

Now sing, "Have a Little Talk with Jesus" as a group.

Now, ladies, we have a very special event or special music. (Have someone or group do something pertinent to the lesson.)

Now the leader will do a brief intro.

We have all heard of Martha and Mary, the sisters of Lazarus who lived in Bethany, just outside Jerusalem. They often invited Jesus and His disciples into their home. They were complex characters, and hopefully by the time we leave here today, we will be able to recognize the lessons God intended for us to learn from these sisters in Christ.

Watch an Elizabeth Etheridge video (or an appropriate intro to Mary and Martha).

9:45–10:15: Scriptures and reflection.

Now we will read the Scriptures that pertain to these two women.

Divide the readings so each group leader reads a portion: Luke 10:38–42, John 11:1–16, John 11:17–44, and John 12:1–8.

We assume Martha was the oldest of the three siblings. There is no mention of parents, so perhaps we can assume they were orphaned. We know, however, that they lived in a house large enough to entertain several people. We also know they had enough money to provide frequently for large numbers of guests.

Martha opened her home several times and seemed to be very comfortable with Jesus. This would indicate that they were good friends. She assumed the role of hostess and ran around to make sure every detail had been taken care of and everything was just right.

This is where we find her in the first passage. She was no shrinking violet when she confronted Jesus. She clearly asked Him, "Don't You care?" She was doing all the work, while Mary, her sister, was sitting around at Jesus' feet. For Martha, her sister's actions were wrong on several fronts. Traditionally women weren't allowed to sit with the men, much less listen to the teachings. It was illegal for women to be taught. Clearly Mary belonged with the women, helping prepare and serve the meal. Martha might have been a little jealous, thinking she was the matriarch of the family and if anyone was going to lounge with the men, it should have been her.

Martha was practical and efficient. She had to be sure her household was running smoothly and her guests were happy. Perhaps she was even embarrassed by Mary's actions, afraid someone would think Mary wasn't being raised properly. Poor Martha—as if she didn't have enough to do but then to add to that she had to be sure her sister was behaving properly.

I am sure we have all been in this situation. There is a little video by Anita Renfroe that seems to sum up a mother's stress in a few seconds. Let's watch it.

Show the Anita Renfroe video on YouTube, "Mom's Song" (or something appropriate and funny that displays the stresses we all face as women).

Now we know and sympathize somewhat with Martha when she got upset. Jesus gently rebuked Martha and basically said, "Leave Mary alone. Mary is paying attention to what is important." This must have hurt a little. At very least Martha must have been confused. Why wasn't Jesus sticking up for her? Some of you will have time in your groups to think about this.

The next recorded account of Martha was after her brother Lazarus died. When she heard that Jesus had arrived, she was the first one to approach Him. We must remember that they were great friends, and Martha knew Jesus shared her grief at the loss of her brother. She again confronted Jesus. Initially, it appeared that she was angry but then she displayed great faith. She told Jesus that she believed God would do anything He asked Him to do. Jesus revealed to Martha that He was the resurrection and the life. He told her that He was the way to eternal life, and she again reaffirmed her faith by telling Him that she believed in Him.

Mary was a thinker or perhaps a dreamer. It has been suggested that she was shy, but I am not totally convinced about that. She was humble and dedicated to Jesus. Nothing is said about how she reacted to Martha's complaint, but she didn't seem to be affected by it.

The next time we see Mary is at the grave of Lazarus with Jesus. When she arrived, she wept openly. This was when Jesus emotionally broke down and wept as well.

Later in His ministry, when Jesus returned to Bethany, Mary again displayed her undying love and devotion to Jesus. She entered the room where Jesus and His disciples had gathered for a meal and anointed his head with expensive perfume. She apparently used very expensive oil that was used typically for embalming bodies. Was it left over from Lazarus's funeral? Was it a gift to her? Or did she use her own money to purchase it? It has been said to be worth a year's salary!

This time her actions were criticized by one of the men, and once again Jesus stuck up for her. He used this opportunity to reveal His death to His disciples.

10:15–11:00: Small work groups—do this in a separate area if one is available. Have paper available for the team leader to record discussion results. Encourage people to use the restroom and get drinks whenever necessary, and make everyone feel comfortable.

Questions for Martha groups

1. What kinds of things did Martha have to do as head of the household?

2. How did that make her feel?

3. What did she want Jesus to do?

4. How did she change by the time Lazarus died?

5. As a group, how can we share our conclusions with the whole group?

If your group wants to create a skit or write a short story, poem, or song that you can present to the entire group, that's great. If not just write the results and be ready to share them when during the sharing time. If some people feel uncomfortable presenting, don't try to shame them into it. Use people who are okay with speaking for the group. Encourage them to be creative.

Leaders, you are to direct the conversation, not take it over. Make your group think. Use your hints from your training, but let the conversation flow as long as it is on topic. If you have time, look over and discuss the Mary questions.

Helpful information for Leaders of the Martha Groups

1. In biblical times, men and women had defined duties. Martha did what was expected of her. Just a few tasks for a typical women's day were as follows:

   - Grinding grain for bread, then mixing, kneading, and baking bread for the day.
   - Purchasing meat at the market or preparing an animal from the household flock for meat to eat, then cooking the meat.
   - Carding, spinning, and weaving threads to make cloth for clothing, beading, and other household uses.
   - Washing and sewing clothing for household members.
   - Drawing the water for the day.
   - Cleaning the house, including washing utensils and dishes.
   - Teaching and disciplining the children of the household.
   - Also, no work was allowed on the Sabbath, so everything had to be done in advance.

2. Tired! Afraid! Competent! Worried! Jealous! Impatient! Scripture doesn't really address how Martha felt. The Scripture points to the familiarity between Martha and Jesus in that she felt comfortable enough to confront Him. This is a connection we need to covet—having such a close personal relationship with Him that we can go to him with any problem, no matter how small.

3. Did she want Jesus to tell Mary to help her? Did she want Him to sympathize with her? Again Scripture doesn't tell us specifically, but how would we feel? How do we feel when there seems to be too much to do? This verse asks, "Jesus, don't You care?" That teaches another powerful lesson that transcends the centuries. We have all wondered that, and yet this question should help us put things in perspective. Was Mary really behaving so badly, or did Martha want to

be in the limelight? Perhaps Martha just wanted to be appreciated or recognized for her contribution. Was she trying to earn her salvation? We need to remember that we can't earn our salvation. Jesus did that for us.

4.   She didn't. In what ways was she the same? Was she more spiritual? If so, how? Scripture next mentions Martha at Lazarus' tomb. She was still a take-charge person. She still confronted Jesus, but she displayed great faith. Jesus revealed to her that He was "the resurrection and the life." Maybe she had spent more time "at His feet" or in the stories. Was her faith in Him as her Savior being displayed stronger than her faith in Him as a friend?

Questions for Mary groups

1. What was it that kept Mary at Jesus' feet?

2. Did Mary care about her proper place in society?

3. Why did Mary break down in front of Jesus at Lazarus's tomb?

4. Why did Mary use expensive oil to wipe Jesus' feet? Did she use something that was hers, or did she go buy it? Why did she go into the room with the men again? Was it just to take care of Jesus? Why did she use her hair to dry His feel?

5. How can we show the entire group what our conclusions were?

Create a skit; select someone to read a short story, poem, or song you have written as a group. If some people feel uncomfortable with presenting, don't try to shame them into it. Get people who are okay with speaking for the group. Encourage them to be creative.

Leaders, you are to direct the conversation, not take it over. Make your group think, use your hints from your training, but let the conversation flow as long as it is on subject. If you have time, look over and discuss the Mary questions.

Helpful Information for the Leaders of the Mary groups

1. Was she lazy? Did she get caught up in the discussion while she was serving? The Scriptures don't answer this question. It has been suggested that perhaps she was helping with the feet washing and just got caught up in the lessons Jesus was teaching. Perhaps she was listening from the corner and tried to be inconspicuous by lying at His feet.

2. Did she even think about what she was doing? Did she care that Martha was doing all the work by herself? Women were never allowed to be taught in the same areas as men. Rabbis were not allowed to instruct women. They had to worship in separate areas and were kept apart unless they were serving the men. This seems to imply that either Mary was very young, because young girls before puberty were allowed to be with the men, or she was so enamored with Jesus's teachings that she didn't care. This part of the Scripture perhaps introduces the new covenant that Jesus came to give us. Women were also part of the change in ancient ritual. Like the Gentiles, they would be allowed an equal participation in the kingdom.

3. Didn't she have the same faith as Martha in knowing that Jesus could help? How do you think she felt when she saw Jesus weep? Again, we need to think about how old Mary was. We know she was younger than Martha. Death was perhaps a little more traumatic. Mary was more emotional. She hadn't experienced as many hard knocks as Martha. She was sheltered as the baby. Most assume their parents were dead, so what did Lazarus's passing mean to Martha and her? Remember, they needed a man in their society to be betrothed and to be escorted into the temple. Scripture doesn't tell us how she felt when she saw Jesus cry. Was she afraid all was really lost? Or was she just sad for Him at the loss of His friend?

4. None of these questions are answered by Scripture. We know Mary loved Jesus on many levels, as a friend, teacher, and perhaps surrogate brother, so she wanted to do something special for Him. After Jesus raised Lazarus, the church leaders were afraid of His power. People were flocking to him, so Mary could have had a feeling that something bad was going to happen. As a young girl she had little or no power, income, or influence. Her only accepted form of worship was to serve, and she did this completely. She gave all she had.

11:00–11:30: Group presentations, sharing, and summation in the sanctuary.

Welcome back. Now we will see what you have done.

Go through all the questions in the discussion and then concentrate on your question results for presentation of the Martha questions and Mary questions. Try to have a large paper pad on an easel and markers to write responses so everyone can see and share.

11:30–11:45: Short presentation 1 (group leader)

God has a plan for our lives, but how many times do we think we know better? He has given us talents so we can complete the things He has given us to do. Martha was doing the job God gave her the talent and ability to do. She was in charge of the household, and that was a lot of work. She may have even taken on other tasks, like baking or shopping, because she wanted them to be done her way. How many times do you set out to wash the floor and then stop to dust a side table, move that dishcloth to the hamper, and rearrange the table setting so before you know it the whole day is gone and the floor hasn't gotten washed? All of those things may have needed to be done, but you have lost your focus. Don't we all let things get in the way of the plan God has for us?

Initially, you can't even know what God wants you to do unless you study His Word. Daily devotional time has to be built into your schedule just like exercise or bathing. Try grabbing your Bible before your feet even hit the floor in the morning. Pick something easy, like Psalms, Proverbs, or the gospels in the beginning so you aren't overwhelmed. Put God first. You don't need to spend a long time studying; ten to fifteen minutes daily is enough to begin with.

Keep your radio on the Christian station and/or bring praise CDs with you in the car. If you have time to jog or go to the gym with ear buds, use Christian music and let God speak to you through these venues.

It will be a simple way to spend time in the spirit and do two things at once, which is what we women do best.

You will be surprised by the calming effect these things will have on you. If you become stressed, the Word and praise will come into your mind and transform you to a peaceful place. God speaks to us through everything we do, and He is always with us.

Jesus told Martha that Mary had made the right choice to learn what He had to teach. Women today don't have to hide their desires to learn the ways of God, but they still have to choose to study. By being here this morning, you have made the right choice. Make a commitment and continue this work.

Jesus went on to tell Martha that the things Mary had chosen wouldn't be taken away from her. The same applies to you. Time spent in study, praise, and the Word will not be taken away from you.

We know all the excuses and have used them: not enough time; the kids have to go to school early; you need to make breakfast. Hear the words of the Lord, make the right choices and the peace that comes with knowledge will not be taken away from you.

We know that God has a plan for us and we don't have to earn our salvation. Nothing we can do will pay the price. We can't make it better because Jesus made it best. He paid the ultimate wage for our sins. All we have to do is ask and we are saved. (Now either sing or listen to, "Jesus Paid It All.")

11:45–12:00: Short motivational woman speaker—personal testimony on an appropriate subject

12: 00–12:15:

Write a letter to yourself. We will mail it to you before the next retreat. Reflect on your Martha and Mary sides or what you are feeling about where you are on your journey. Make a resolution to spend more time in the Word and prayer. Then in the future you can see how you did. If you don't want to write a letter, this will be a reflection time. Listen to the music, watch the video, and take time to fill out the questionnaire.

12:15–12:30: Praise and questions or comments

Thank everyone who helped. Sing a praise song and give a prayer of parting!

Come Meet
Naomi and Ruth

Welcome to the study of Naomi and Ruth. This is intended to inspire women to understand themselves and how they relate to this mother-in-law and daughter-in-law. We used two reference guides: the *NIV Study Bible*[3] and *Women of the Bible.*[4]

This study can be used by groups of any size. It is designed for women to learn and share in a limited amount of time (three to four hours) but can be adapted to stretch into a full day by adding a lunch and lengthening discussion times. It allows for creativity, sharing, reflection, and spiritual education.

Organizers are encouraged to get speakers and singers, use electronics, and/or stick to the basics and sing the old familiar hymns. This study allows the organization the freedom to tailor the study to their own group and yet share the blessings of the biblical message of Naomi and Ruth. This study will use the entire book of Ruth and will be complex and diversified. There is a lot of material and subject matter to cover, and the historical traditions of that time are very important to add to the study.

---

[3] Copyright 1973, 1978, 1984 by International Bible Society. Zondervan Publishing, Grand Rapids, Michigan.
[4] Ann Spangler and Jean E. Syswerda, *Women of the Bible.* (Grand Rapids, MI: Zondervan Publishing, 1999).

Agenda

To dress it up, use the logo you selected and Ruth 2:12: "May the Lord repay you for what you have done. May you be richly rewarded by the Lord God of Israel under whose wings you have come to take refuge."

9:00–9:30: Welcome, coffee, registration—relax and enjoy greeting everyone

9:30–9:45: Opening, introduction, and praise in the sanctuary (if possible)

9:45–10:15: Scriptures and reflection

10:15–11:00: Small work groups

11:00–11:30: Group presentations, sharing, and summation

11:40–1:50: Short motivational woman speaker (or two)

12:00–12:15: Letter-writing time and/or private devotional time

12:15–12:30: Conclusion, praise songs, and prayer

Welcome, ladies, to our women's retreat. We will be studying Naomi and Ruth. We'd like to open with a song. If you know it, help us sing! Remember, these are praise songs, so don't be afraid to get loud, clap, or raise your hands. Be happy this is our time to put everything aside except the Spirit. Let Him come and give us what we need.

Next introduce the committee and bring everyone up front to sing, "This Is the Day."

Housekeeping Announcements, Folder Instruction, and Scheduling

This morning we pray we will get a better understanding of the lessons God wants us to learn from Naomi and Ruth. Before we get started, we have a few housekeeping and scheduling items to deal with. When you registered, you were given a folder. Inside you should have a schedule for this morning and the book of Ruth printed out, which is the Scripture we are basing our study on. A questionnaire is included for you to fill out at the end of the day to help us plan for the next retreat. Let us know what you liked and what didn't like. We want you to tell all. On the other side of the folder is a piece of paper that will be used to write a letter to a friend who has been with you through thick and thin. Whether you mail it or not is up to you. This will also be a time of personal reflection so if you don't want to write a letter, be prepared to be alone with yourself and God.

Bathrooms are located _____.

The committee has worked very hard on this agenda, and we hope to keep to the times as much as possible. We would like to invite you to stay for a short lunch after the retreat. Without further ado, let's get this amazing day started with prayer.

Pray: Father, as we meet today, may we learn the things You would have us learn about Ruth and Naomi. May we become stronger and better daughters, mothers, mothers-in-law, daughters-in-law, friends, and Christian women. Help us to share with each other and give of ourselves in Your service. In Jesus' name, amen.

9:45–10:15: Scriptures and reflection Naomi and Ruth. Scripture: The book of Ruth.

There is a rather long (nine minutes) video on YouTube called "Naomi's Story" by truestorymaker. It's modern and nice and may be a good beginning.

> The author of the book of Ruth is unknown, but we think it was written about three hundred years after the actual events. It is estimated that these things took place around 1360 BC during the time of the judges. Mosaic Law was followed during this part of Jewish history. These rules are found in the first five books of the Bible called the Pentateuch, which includes but is not limited to the Ten Commandments.
>
> Naomi, her husband, and their two sons left their home during a time of great famine and went to Moab, where they hoped to find a better life. Naomi's husband died, and the boys married girls from Moab. Then during the next ten years, the sons died as well. Naomi and her daughters-in-law, Ruth and Orpah, were left alone with a very bleak outlook for the future. Naomi heard that the famine was over in Judah and decided to return to Bethlehem, the city of her birth. She was so sad and discouraged with the way her life had turned out that she didn't want Ruth and Orpah to suffer with her, so she released them from their obligation to her and sent them back to their families. She hoped they would be able to find someone who would marry them in their hometowns, even though they were widows. Tradition taught her that she could be taken into the family of one of her husband's brothers, if they would have her. She was beyond childbearing years so she was of little use to any man, but she did have land that belonged to the husband to use as a bargaining chip.
>
> Although the girls seemed to want to stay with Naomi, once she told them what her prospects would be, Orpah returned to her birth

family. Ruth, however, vowed to stay with Naomi, and together they returned to Bethlehem. They arrived during harvest time, and it was necessary for them to get supplies put away for the winter. Naomi's land had not been planted so they were forced to live like paupers and glean the fields for whatever leftovers they could find. Naomi knew her brother-in-law, Boaz, was a decent man and recommended that Ruth use his field to collect whatever grains she could. The laws of Moses required that landowners leave some grain on the ground for the poor to collect as they harvested the bulk for themselves. It was common practice to have strangers following the paid workers. I was unusual, however, to see a foreigner such as Ruth in the fields.

When Ruth pledged to follow Naomi to Judah, she vowed to take up the Jewish ways, rebuke the Moabite deities, and worship the Jewish God. Boaz met Ruth as she was working in the field. He told her to stay near his slave girls and to only work in his field. This would secure her safety. Boaz warned his men to leave her alone and arranged for them to leave a little extra grain for her. Ruth thanked Boaz and later that night told Naomi about his kindness.

Naomi told Ruth that Boaz was a close relative and it might be possible for him to be their kinsman-redeemer. A kinsman-redeemer was responsible for protecting the interests of needy members of the extended family. This is a pivotal point in the story because Naomi is filled with hope that Boaz will help them in the future.

As the harvest came to an end, the men worked long hours separating the wheat from the chaff. It was generally a time of celebration and male bonding. They celebrated and after a big meal, found a spot on the threshing room floor and spent the night guarding their grain. At this time Naomi suggested that Ruth go to Boaz and appeal to his sense of duty or obligation. This was an unusual suggestion because it would appear somewhat improper. Ruth was encouraged to go sleep at Boaz's feet, and when he woke, she was to approach him with the idea of taking care of her and Naomi. This was a big risk on Ruth's part, but Boaz knew of her sacrifice to stay with Naomi and provide for her, so he accepted her offer and began the process to become their kinsman-redeemer.

There was an older brother who had first rights to Naomi's land, so Boaz had to go to him and ask if he wanted to take on the responsibilities of Ruth and Naomi. The brother wanted her land, but according to law, in order to keep the land, he would have had to marry Ruth. He was not willing to do this so he relinquished his rights to Boaz.

Ruth and Boaz were married and produced a son named Obed. Naomi was so happy that she had a grandson, an heir. She was the envy of the village women, who said that Ruth was better to her than seven sons. Obed was a direct descendant to the line of David and to Jesus Christ, our Lord and Savior.

10:15–11:00: Small group work where props, paper, etc., should be available. Encourage people to use the restroom and get drinks whenever necessary, and make your group feel comfortable.

Questions about Naomi

1. Think about and discuss what it must have been like for Naomi and her family living in famine conditions and how hard their decision must have been to leave their hometown to move to Moab. What kinds of things did they have to consider?

2. After Naomi had lost her husband, her sons were obligated to care for her in their homes. She lived with them for approximately ten years before both sons died too. How difficult was it for Naomi to have to be practical about her survival during that devastating time of mourning?

3. Naomi's name means "pleasant," and yet when she returned to Bethlehem, she told the ladies that they should call her Mara, which means "bitter." Talk about a time when perhaps you were in a position that you couldn't see your way out of. The women reminded her to "Praise the Lord." Read Ruth 4:14–15, and be ready to share a time when you knew the Lord had not left you.

4. God's faithfulness is shown in Naomi's story. No matter how depressed she was, God had a plan for her that was fulfilled. Think about times when you've come through a bad time, only to be part of a miracle. Discuss ways to reach out to others and remind them that God has a plan and "He will renew and sustain them."

5. Pick a way to demonstrate to the group the answer from one of the questions above. Each Naomi group should take a different question.

Leaders, you are to direct the conversation, not take it over. Make your group think and use your hints from your training, but let the conversation flow as long as it is on subject. If there is time, look over and discuss the Ruth questions.

Helpful Hints for Leaders of Naomi Groups

1. Discuss famine and the dangers it presents to life. Talk about leaving home and the things that are familiar to move to somewhere strange where you don't know the language, customs, gods, etc. Elimelech, Naomi's husband, was the ultimate decision maker, but what kinds of things did Naomi have to deal with?

2. Think of how Naomi must have felt having to rely on her sons to take care of her. Then when they were killed, she was virtually alone with the two wives. Moab was their home so they knew the area better than she.

3. We all know in our hearts that God won't forsake us. We have the promise in Psalm 71:20 and Joel 2:25–26. Sometimes we have trouble recognizing His presence with us. Try to get your group to open up about their times of doubt and look into that time for God's presence. Remember the "Footsteps" poem where God tells the person when he was in his darkest hour, there was only one set of footsteps because God was carrying him.

4. Think about times in your life when someone or something has come to you when you least expect it and has truly changed you. Remember people who have crossed your path that you can thank or just reach out to. Maybe it is people you have lost contact with and you would just like to let them know how much them being in your life meant to you.

Questions about Ruth

1. Ruth's name means "friendship." How does this fit her personality? What are some reasons why she wanted to stay with Naomi and go to a strange land?

2. Ruth was a very young widow, but she demonstrated strong character and will. How do you think she felt when everyone talked about her and how she changed her religion and lived in a strange culture just to support her mother-in-law?

3. Ruth was a Moabite. Her people worshipped the god Chemosh, who was a cruel, bloodthirsty deity. Do you think she was surprised to discover that Naomi's God was generous, loyal, and loving? Based on the cruelty that Ruth must have witnessed in Moab, do you think that had anything to do with her not appearing to be scared and doing whatever Naomi asked her to do?

4. Ruth was not used to the laws of Moses and yet she trusted Naomi when she told her to approach Boaz alone. She was risking her life to approach him in the manner she did. Do you think she was in love with Boaz? Was she comfortable with him and grateful that he tried to protect her in the field? Or was she just looking for someone to take care of her and Naomi?

5. Pick a way to demonstrate to the group the answer from one of the questions above.

Leaders, you are to direct the conversation, not take it over. Make your group think and use your hints from your training, but let the conversation flow as long as it is on subject. If there is time, look over and discuss the Naomi questions.

Helpful Hints for the Leaders of Ruth Groups

1. Think about Ruth's relationship to Naomi. Perhaps she wasn't close with her own mother or her family disowned her for marrying a Jew. Women of these times were totally dependent on their husbands. Remember, Ruth was a widow too.

2. Ask if your participants have ever had to live in a strange place where they didn't understand the language or any of the customs, like military families or missionaries. Talk about how hard it would be to not know the value of money or what traditions were acceptable or unacceptable. This was a very rigid society, and people were stoned for the slightest infraction.

3. Ancient deities of that time were often cruel, warmonger types. Sacrificing children and taking a person's heart while it was still beating to offer it to the gods was commonplace. Imagine how Ruth felt when she heard about Naomi's loving God. Think of the time when you first accepted Christ as your Savior and how relieved and content you felt. Remember how enthusiastic you were to obey the laws and come closer to the family of God.

4. The Jewish traditions were unfamiliar to Ruth so she had to rely on Naomi's opinion as to what was proper. There have been many suggestions that Ruth behaved in an improper manner, but remember God had a plan for her. Her faithfulness to Naomi and God led her to be a direct descendant of Jesus Christ.

11:00–12:00: Group presentations, sharing, and summation in the sanctuary. Go through all the questions in the discussion and then concentrate on your question results for presentation.

Suggestions for summation after the group presentations:

1. Have someone talk about living in another country, how she felt, how things were different, etc.

2. As women we share some common bonds. Many of us are drawn to each other by commonality. Think about a time in your life when you stepped out of your comfort zone and "got through it" only to feel stronger after it was done.

3. Show a video about Mother Theresa (there is a bio of her life only a few minutes long). Maybe an open discussion about how she felt going to India and being stoned for her work.

12: 00–12:15:

> Write a letter to someone who has stuck by you or who helped in some way. Reflect on Naomi and Ruth, or what you are feeling about your hardships, your loyalties, and your faith. Make a resolution to spend more time in the Word and prayer. It doesn't matter if you mail this letter or not; the important part of this is a short time of reflection. If you don't want to write a letter this will be a reflection time. Listen to the music, watch the video, and take time to fill out the questionnaire.

12:15–12:30: Praise and questions or comments

Thank everyone who helped. Sing a praise song and say a prayer of parting!

Come Meet
Mary and Elizabeth

Welcome to the study of Mary, the mother of Jesus, and Elizabeth, the mother of John the Baptist. This is intended to inspire women to understand themselves and how they relate to these women. I used the following reference guides: *NIV Study Bible* and *Women of the Bible*.

This study can be used by groups of any size. It is designed for women to learn and share in a limited amount of time (three to four hours) but can be adapted to stretch into a full day by adding a lunch and lengthening discussion times. It allows creativity, sharing, reflection, and spiritual education.

Organizers are encouraged to get speakers or singers, use electronics, and/or stick to the basics and sing the old familiar hymns. It allows the organization the freedom to tailor the study to its own group and yet share the blessings of the biblical message of Mary and Elizabeth. This study uses references from 1 Samuel and the gospels Mathew, Luke, and John. They are to be read in the specific order set out to complete the story of these women. There is no way in a few short hours that you could completely know these women or draw all the conclusions about their lives and the tasks they were given by God to do, but this will open the thought process into an important piece of the plan God had for their lives.

Agenda

To dress it up, use the logo you selected and
Luke 1:41–42: "When Elizabeth heard Mary's greeting, the
baby leaped in her womb, and Elizabeth was filled with the
Holy Spirit. In a loud voice she exclaimed: 'Blessed are you
among women and blessed is the child you will bear!'"

9:00–9:30: Welcome, coffee, registration—relax and enjoy greeting everyone

9:30–9:45: Opening, introduction, and praise in the sanctuary (if possible)

9:45–10:15: Scriptures and reflection

10:15–11:00: Small work groups

11:00–11:30: Group presentations, sharing, and summation

11:40–11:50: Short motivational woman speaker (or two)

12: 00–12:15: Letter-writing time and/or private devotional time

12:15–12:30: Conclusion, praise songs, and prayer

Welcome, ladies, to our women's retreat about Elizabeth and Mary. We'd like to begin with prayer. Father God, we ask that You accept us as we are today. We come with problems, worries, and concerns. We come with hope, with praise, and with rejoicing that we can come closer to You this morning. Send Your Holy Spirit to bless us as we learn what You would have us learn, worship as You would have us worship, and share as You would have us share. We ask this in Jesus' name. Amen.

We'd like to start out by introducing the retreat team. These ladies have given their time and talents to put all of this together, and once I've announced all of them and they stand, let's give them a round of applause.

Let's get going. We'd like to open with a couple of songs. You should know these, so help us sing! Remember, they are praise songs so don't be afraid to get loud, clap, or raise your hands. Be happy. This is our time to put everything aside except the Spirit. Let Him come into us and give us what we need.

All the retreat team should go up front to sing, "This Is the Day" and "Come, Now Is the Time to Worship."

Housekeeping Announcements, Folder Instruction, and Scheduling

This morning we hope to get a better understanding of the lessons God wants us to learn from Mary and Elizabeth. However, we have a few housekeeping and scheduling items to deal with. When you registered, you were given a folder. Inside you should have a schedule for this morning; you also have the Scripture printed out that we are basing our study on. A questionnaire is included for you to fill out at the end of the day to help us plan for the next retreat. Let us know what you liked and what didn't like. We want you to tell us anything you want to share. How can we do this better?

On the other side of the folder is a piece of paper. If you look at the schedule, between twelve and twelve fifteen we have set aside time for you to spend with you. If you choose, you can write yourself another letter. This will be the time to do that. But if you aren't comfortable, use this time for personal reflection or just to sit quietly and listen to God. We will be asking you to separate and find a quiet corner of the sanctuary so you aren't sitting next to anyone. If you choose to write to yourself about things you learned today or something you need to remind yourself about in three months, we will mail the letters to you, so address the envelope to where you will be at that time. There will be some inspirational videos and music playing. Be looking forward to that respite.

Bathrooms are located _____.

The committee has worked very hard on this agenda, and we hope to keep to the times as much as possible. We invite you to stay for a short lunch after the retreat. Without further ado, let's get this amazing day started.

9:45–10:15:

As we have done before, we are going to be looking at two amazing biblical women, Elizabeth, the mother of John the Baptist, and Mary, the mother of Jesus. They are not paired as often as the others we have studied, but I think you will see that their stories are quite similar.

Here is a little background before we read the Scriptures. During these times, the Old Testament was the only guide or rule book the Jews had to live by. The Scriptures predicted the coming of a messiah, and everyone was anxiously waiting for that promise to be fulfilled.

After angels visited Elizabeth's husband in the temple and Mary at her home, they knew they had been chosen by God to do amazing things.

Both women were given the beautiful gift of sons. This gift would prove to be one of great joy and great pain. Elizabeth and Mary were very devout women, but women of those times were not educated in the Scriptures the same way as men. They faithfully attended services in the temple but were kept out of many of the theology discussions. Everyone, however, knew of the promised messiah. It was the good news that they were waiting and praying for to deliver them once again out of bondage. One reference says that all the women of child-bearing age were hoping to be the one chosen to birth the messiah. Imagine how Mary and Elizabeth must have felt to realize that they were not only going to witness this event but that they had also been chosen to play a very huge part in the next chapter of God's plan.

The Scriptures and reflection about Elizabeth and Mary are as follows: Elizabeth, Luke 1:5–25, 56–80, and Mary, Luke 1:26–45.

Before we watch a video about the Magnificat, called Mary's Song, which is found Luke 1:47–55, we'd like you to listen carefully to Hannah's prayer or song, which was recorded sometime around 930 BC in 1 Samuel 2:1. Let's see how close Mary's words echo those of Hannah. Now let's see the video about Mary's song, the Magnificat. Continuing to round out Mary's story, we close with John 19:25–27.

One of your jobs as we go into small groups is to make two lists: *How are Mary and Elizabeth alike? How are Mary and Elizabeth different?*

There will also be questions to contemplate about Mary if you are on the Mary table and questions to contemplate about Elizabeth if you are on the Elizabeth table. Are these amazing women like us? Well, in one way, they are, of course, because we are all amazing. Right?

10:15–11:00: Small group work, where props, paper, etc., should be available. Encourage people to use the restroom and get drinks whenever necessary, and make your group feel comfortable.

Questions about Mary

Have the ladies introduce themselves around the table. Writing on a legal pad, make a list of how Mary and Elizabeth were alike. Then make a list of how Mary and Elizabeth were different.

1. How did Mary feel about the visit from the angel?

2. Why did Mary go to visit Elizabeth?

3. Why did she stay until after John was born?

4. Do you think she had any idea what her life would be like as the mother of Jesus?

Leaders, you are to direct the conversation, not take it over. Make your group think and use your hints from your training, but let the conversation flow as long as it is on subject. If you have time look at the Elizabeth questions and discuss those.

Helpful Hints for Leaders of Mary Groups

Alike: If you need some help, here are a few ideas. They were both chosen by God. They were related (cousins). They were both pregnant. Angels announced their pregnancies. They were both surprised and afraid about their pregnancies. An angel named their babies. An angel visited their husbands. Their sons were men of God. Both of their sons apparently offended the government of Rome. Both of their sons died tragic deaths at a young age.

Different: If you need some help, here are a few ideas. They lived about sixty miles apart. There was a great age difference. Their marital status was different. Elizabeth was overjoyed from the beginning after waiting so many years to conceive where Mary no doubt wasn't thinking about a baby at all until her marriage ceremony was over. Although Mary was visited by an angel and got to ask questions, Elizabeth never saw an angel. Elizabeth's pregnancy occurred about six months before Mary's. We assume Mary stayed for John's birth, but there are no details as to his birth whereas with Jesus' birth there are volumes recorded.

1. Get input. Scared? Honored? Angry?

2. Did she need advice from the older women? Was it just a feeling that Elizabeth would understand? Did she get a hint from the angel?

3. Did Mary feel safe with Elizabeth? Was it a place she could rest away from wondering eyes?

4. Did she know the Scriptures? Isaiah 53:5 tells of the messiah's death.

Questions about Elizabeth

Have the ladies introduce themselves around the table. Writing on a legal pad, make a list of how Mary and Elizabeth were alike. Then make a list of how Mary and Elizabeth were different.

1. How do you think Elizabeth felt when her husband came home and couldn't speak but conveyed to her that they were going to have a baby?

2. Why was Elizabeth's reaction to Mary pregnancy so different than we would have expected? How could she have suspected that Mary was going to give birth to the Messiah?

3. Elizabeth knew John was to be a prophet; do you think she had any idea that he would be killed at a young age as well?

Leaders, you are to direct the conversation, not take it over. Make your group think and use your hints from your training, but let the conversation flow as long as it is on subject. If you have time, look at the Mary questions and discuss those.

Helpful Hints for leaders of Elizabeth Groups

Alike: If you need some help, here are a few ideas. They were both chosen by God. They were related (cousins). They were both pregnant. Angels announced their pregnancies. They were both surprised and afraid about their pregnancies. An angel named their babies. An angel visited their husbands. Their sons were men of God. Both of their sons apparently offended the government of Rome. Both of their sons died tragic deaths at a young age.

Different: If you need some help, here are a few ideas. They lived about sixty miles apart. There was a great age difference. Their marital status was different. Elizabeth was overjoyed from the beginning after waiting so many years to conceive where Mary no doubt wasn't thinking about a baby at all until her marriage ceremony was over. Although Mary was visited by an angel and got to ask questions, Elizabeth never saw an angel. Elizabeth's pregnancy occurred about six months before Mary's. We assume Mary stayed for John's birth, but there are no details as to his birth whereas with Jesus' birth there are volumes recorded.

1. Remember, she was older and considered barren. Perhaps she was scared or unbelieving. (Scripture says she didn't doubt.)

2. She knew her own circumstance was impossible in the natural, so why should she question Mary? She was older and wiser. She wanted to mentor Mary and help her.

3. Elizabeth was educated in the Scriptures. Most prophets didn't fare well. She knew they were of the family of temple workers so John would be turned over to the church for education and his life's work would be spiritual.

11:00–12:00: Group presentations, sharing, and summation in the sanctuary. Go through all the questions in the discussion and then concentrate of your question results for presentation.

Welcome back. Sing the hymn, "Have Thine Own Way, Lord."

Let's get started on the two questions we all discussed and see how many similarities we had. Get a tripod and large pad. Have one person record responses. Okay, now what was different?

For Mary, how did she feel about the visit from the angel? Why did Mary go to visit Elizabeth and stay until after John was born? What did you conclude about Mary's intuition about her future and the future of her son?

For Elizabeth, how do you think she felt when her husband came home and couldn't speak but conveyed to her that they were going to have a baby? Why was Elizabeth's reaction to Mary's pregnancy so different than expected? How could she have suspected that Mary was going to give birth to the Messiah? What did you think about Elizabeth's knowledge that John was to be a prophet? Do you think she had any idea that he would be killed at a young age?

Have a testimony from one of the ladies or a spiritual speaker focusing on a pertinent subject, such as following God. Has He ever asked you to do something uncomfortable?

12:00–12:15:

Write a letter to yourself. We will mail it to you before the next retreat. Reflect on Elizabeth and Mary or what you are feeling about where you are on your journey. Make a resolution to spend more time in the Word and prayer. Then in the future you can see how you did. If you don't want to write a letter, this will be a reflection time. Listen to the music, watch the video, and take time to fill out the questionnaire.

12:15–12:30: Praise and questions or comments

Thank everyone who helped. Sing a praise song and say a prayer of parting!

Conclusions

This workbook is designed as simply as possible to encourage women to study the Bible. It gives them time for relaxation, inspiration, interaction, and learning. Sharing these Bible lessons will help to quench a thirst for religious knowledge and empower women to realize they are the backbone of society.

Mary and Martha teach us to focus on what is really important. We need to help and serve others, but God has to take first place in our lives. His plan for us is what we should avidly seek. There are so many facets of this story, but most important is that fact that Jesus related to Mary and Martha on a personal level. He gently chastised Martha to let Mary learn and then He wept with them at the death of their brother. This closeness reminds us that our God is personal. He cares about our problems, and He is there when we need Him.

Naomi and Ruth encourage us to use the strength and diversity we have as women to overcome all odds. They were alone, and yet they found hope in an impossible situation and exhibited the tenacity to overcome obstacles. Ruth looked to her mother-in-law for advice, showed respect to her elders, and honored her commitment. Together they relied on the God of Israel to stay with them and show them the plan He had for their lives.

Elizabeth and Mary were truly blessed among women of all generations. They accepted God's plan without question or fear. Strength and courage are displayed in every part of their story. Modern women who find themselves in similar situations, whether they are naive, educated, engaged, long married, infertile, or pregnant, can relate to Elizabeth and Mary. Their stories are similar in servitude, acceptance, and dedication. They encourage us to let God guide us and to trust in what He has asked us to do.

Printed in the United States
By Bookmasters